W9-CHM-469

Nigeria

Mary N. Oluonye

🌿 Carolrhoda Books / Minneapolis

Photo Acknowledgments

Photos, maps, and artworks are used courtesy of: Laura Westlund, pp. 1, 2-3, 4, 6, 11, 19, 25, 33, 38; © Bruce Paton, Panos Pictures, pp. 5, 24, 35 (top), 44; © Sara Leigh Lewis, Panos Pictures, pp. 6-7; Hutchison Library, pp. 6 (bottom), 12, 14, 32; © James Morris, Panos Pictures, pp. 8, 23 (bottom), 28 (top), 35 (bottom); © Mary N. Oluonye, pp. 9, 26 (bottom), 28 (bottom), 30, 33, 40; Food and Agriculture Organization, p. 10; © Trip/Max Moore, p. 13; © Trip/J. Okwesa, pp. 15, 17; © Phil Porter, pp. 16, 18 (bottom); © Carol Barker from A *Family in Nigeria*, by Carol Barker (A & C Black), pp. 18 (top), 20, 21, 29, 39 (bottom), 45; © Trip/J. Highet, pp. 22, 31, 34-35, 34 (bottom), 37; © Betty Press, Panos Pictures, p. 23 (top); © Marcus rose, Panos Pictures, pp. 26-27 ; © Lois Coren, Root Resources, p. 36 (top); © Trip/M. Jelliffe, p. 36 (bottom); Library of Congress, p. 39 (top); © David Cannon/All Sport, p. 41 (bottom); © Ben Radford/All Sport, p. 41 (top); © Martin Adler, Panos Pictures, p. 42. Cover photo of Nigerian market © James Morris, Panos Pictures.

Carolrhoda Books
A division of Lerner Publishing Group, Inc.
241 First Avenue North
Minneapolis, Minnesota 55401 U.S.A.

Website address: www.lernerbooks.com

Words in **bold type** are explained in a glossary that begins on p. 44.

Library of Congress Cataloging-in-Publication Data

Oluonye, Mary N.
    Nigeria / by Mary N. Oluonye.
        p.   cm. — (Globe-trotters club)
    Includes index.
    Summary: An overview of Nigeria, emphasizing its cultural aspects.
    ISBN 978–1–57505–113–0 (lib. bdg.: alk. paper)
    1. Nigeria—Juvenile literature. [1. Nigeria.] I. Title. II. Series.
    Globe-trotters club (series)
    DT515.22.O49 1998
    966.9—DC21   97-16567

Manufactured in the United States of America
2 – CG – 7/15/10

Contents

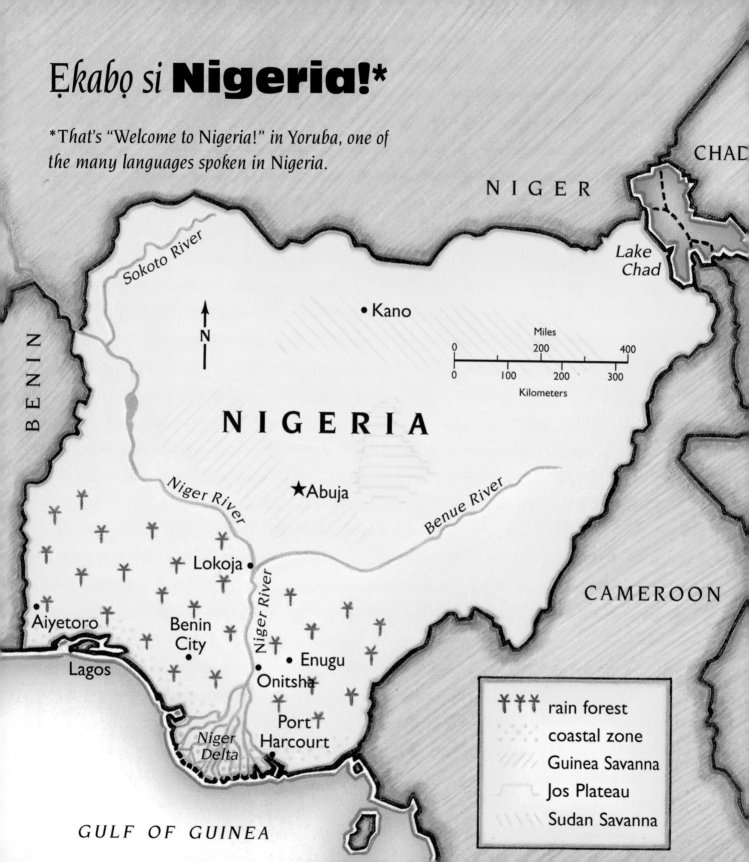

Ẹ̀kàbọ̀ si **Nigeria!***

*That's "Welcome to Nigeria!" in Yoruba, one of the many languages spoken in Nigeria.

CHAD

NIGER

Lake Chad

Sokoto River

• Kano

BENIN

N

NIGERIA

Miles
0   200   400
0   100   200   300
Kilometers

Niger River

★Abuja

Benue River

CAMEROON

+ Lokoja •

Niger River

Aiyetoro

Benin City

• Enugu
Onitsha

Lagos

Port Harcourt

Niger Delta

GULF OF GUINEA

✝✝✝ rain forest
coastal zone
Guinea Savanna
Jos Plateau
Sudan Savanna

Nigeria is one of the biggest nations on the continent of Africa. The country has 36 states and is home to more than 115 million people!

To find Nigeria on a map of Africa, locate the bulge along the western coast that juts into the Atlantic Ocean. Nigeria is tucked into the bottom of that bulge. Niger and Chad are Nigeria's northern neighbors. To the west is Benin, and to the east is Cameroon. The warm waters of the gulf of Guinea wash against Nigeria's southern border.

Mangrove trees grow in swamps, places where salty ocean water meets freshwater. This mangrove swamp is near Lagos.

Fast Facts about Nigeria

Name: Federal Republic of Nigeria
Area: 356,669 square miles
Population: Approximately 115 million
Major Rivers: Niger, Benue, Sokoto, Kaduna, Gongola
Major Lakes: Lake Chad
Highest Point: Dimlang (2,700 feet)
Lowest Point: Sea Level
Capital City: Abuja (Before 1991 the capital was Lagos.)
Other Major Cities: Lagos, Ibadan, Kano, Port Harcourt, Onitsha
Official Language: English
Monetary Unit: Naira

A Bird's-eye **View**

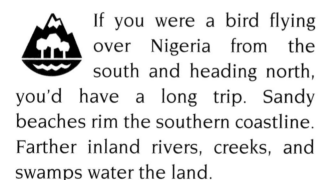

If you were a bird flying over Nigeria from the south and heading north, you'd have a long trip. Sandy beaches rim the southern coastline. Farther inland rivers, creeks, and swamps water the land.

Before flying too far, you'd begin to see miles and miles of green, because southern Nigeria is covered with dense **tropical rain forests**. In some spots, mahogany and iroko trees grow so thick and close together that they stop sunlight from ever touching the forest floor. To the gorillas, chimpanzees, baboons, and

6

(Left) **In this rain forest in southwestern Nigeria, some trees reach 150 feet in height. That's taller than 3 telephone poles stacked on top of each other!** (Bottom left) **Heavy rains drench the Jos Plateau in central Nigeria.**

Before you land, you'll fly over the hot, dry region along Nigeria's northern border. This area is not far from the Sahara **Desert.** Not much grows here. And from the air, the ground looks red. No kidding! Tiny bits of a metal called iron make the dirt look rusty red.

monkeys that live in the forest, the tangled, leafy branches are like one giant playground.

The land begins to rise slowly as you continue your flight northward. In the middle of the country, the trees thin out, and a wide, open, grassy area known as the **savanna** takes over. Farmers grow crops and raise cows and sheep here.

Sidetrack

From 1861 to 1960, the British controlled Nigeria as a **colony.** They introduced the English language, which later became the country's official language.

Getting Carried Away

Many streams join to form this waterfall.

Take a look at the map of Nigeria on page four. See the two rivers that form a wide "Y" across the land? These are the two most important rivers in Nigeria. The Niger River begins in Guinea and enters Nigeria from the west. The Benue River is the Niger's main **tributary,** a smaller river that flows into a bigger one. The Benue River cuts across the eastern half of the country. The two rivers become one at Lokoja and then continue southward as the Niger River.

As the Niger moves across central Nigeria, the river drops from higher to lower ground, creating beautiful waterfalls. In other spots, though, where the land is flat, the Niger River

Nigerians use the **Niger River** for bathing and washing clothes.

Swept Away

Rivers carry more than mud. Uprooted plants, fish, and other tiny water animals also go along for the ride. When the Niger empties into the gulf, the plants and animals that don't wriggle free are buried under layers of mud. Over time, these living things break down to create oil. British petroleum companies first discovered oil in the Niger Delta in 1956. Life changed for many Nigerians in 1960, when Nigeria became independent and gained control of the oil business. Nigeria was quickly transformed from a farming country into a wealthier nation dependent on the oil business. These days Nigeria has the largest supply of oil south of the Sahara Desert.

travels slowly. During the rainy season, the river floods. It swallows up dirt tracks and carries away topsoil from farms.

What happens to all that swirling mud? The river dumps all the soil into a giant fan-shaped area called the Niger Delta that forms just as the river spills into the Gulf of Guinea.

Who Lives **in Nigeria?**

School's out! These school kids laugh and play on their way back to their home village of Aiyetoro.

People from more than 300 **ethnic groups,** that's who! And each group has its own customs, beliefs, and language. Sounds confusing, doesn't it? For many Nigerians, it has been.

Before the British took control of Nigeria in 1861, the Hausa, the Yoruba, the Igbo, and the Fulani— the main ethnic groups in Nigeria— each ruled themselves in separate areas of present-day Nigeria. The

Hausa and the Fulani controlled the north, the Yoruba dominated the southwest, and the Igbo lived in the southeast. The British combined these groups and several smaller groups into one colony. Suddenly they were all supposed to be Nigerians, even though they had completely different histories, cultures, and languages. Living together peacefully didn't happen overnight, either. In fact, Nigerians are still working on getting along better.

But most Nigerians have one thing in common—they speak English, the country's official language. People use English in schools, businesses, and government offices, but at home they prefer their own Nigerian language. Hausa speak Hausa, Yoruba talk to one another in Yoruba . . . well, you get the idea.

Pidgin English

Pidgin English is another form of language widely used in Nigeria. It combines simple English phrases with bits from Nigerian languages. Pidgin sounds very different from standard English, yet many visitors, especially children, are able to understand it. Some even learn a few phrases for the trip home. Here are a few examples.

Pidgin	English
Whetin you want sabe?	What do you want to know?
Whetin you want chop?	What do you want to eat?
Make we dey go!	Let's go!

U*p* **North**

Some Nigerians can guess at another's ethnic group just by looking at the person's clothing, coloring, height, or build. And, because most ethnic groups have stayed put since the British colonized Nigeria, where a Nigerian lives can also give ethnic clues.

If you were to visit a Nigerian girl from the northern city of Kano, chances are that she is either a Hausa or a Fulani. How would you know if she were one or the other? Both groups tend to have lighter skin than Nigerians from other groups, but if she braided her hair into elaborate designs, she'd probably be a Fulani. The Hausa and Fulani live north of the Niger and Benue Rivers. Of all Nigerians, these two groups have had the most contact with their Arab neighbors to the

A Hausa man from northern Nigeria holds his daughter on his lap. Many Nigerians wear hats or head scarves to keep cool under the hot sun.

north. The Arabs introduced the Hausa and the Fulani to the Islamic religion. People who follow this religion are called Muslims.

The Hausa have lived in northern Nigeria, Niger, and Chad as farmers, craftworkers, and traders for more than a thousand years. The Fulani traveled into the area about 800 years ago. They were nomads—people who move from one place to another looking for water and grazing land for their animals. Many Fulani still live this way.

A Fulani man rounds up his cattle and sheep in the north's dry and dusty climate.

Two Yoruba women share a joke while tending to their cloth booth at the marketplace. They are wearing gowns and heads scarves made from the cloth they sell.

Down **South**

South of Lokoja, the Niger River divides the Yoruba in the southwest from the Igbo in the southeast. Say your pen pal from Lagos, a big city in southwestern Nigeria, sends a picture of himself. He's tall and skinny. Bet he's Yoruba! The Yoruba people believe that their ancestors came from Egypt in northern Africa many hundreds of years ago. Although many Yoruba are farmers, most live in towns and drive to their farms each day. They grow cacao beans, yams, peanuts, and corn. But not all Yoruba are farmers—some make a living from fishing.

A person from the southeastern town of Enugu is likely to be an Igbo. The Igbo accepted British culture more readily than the Yoruba, Hausa, or Fulani did, so southeastern Nigeria is the least traditional part of the country. In colonial times, the British hired the Igbo for important government jobs. These days many Igbos are doctors or lawyers, while others work in business or trade.

Rain or Shine

Rain or sunshine describes most weather forecasts in Nigeria. Here's a tip—carry an umbrella from March through November because during these months, it rains almost every day.

Nigerians who live in the south are much more likely to get wet than those who live in the north. Why? Because the south is closer to the Atlantic Ocean, where rain-filled clouds often form. The north, on the other hand, is closer to the dry heat of the Sahara Desert. The dry season hits in December. It's got company, too, the **harmattan.** These hot, dry winds blow from the northeast, carrying rust-red dust across Nigeria. Daytime temperatures during the dry season are hot all over the country, but especially in the north where the air is so dry. Nigerians rub lotion on their skin and lips to prevent chapping.

In Onitsha, a medium-sized town on the Niger in southeastern Nigeria, people use boats to get from one place to another.

Clothing **Clues**

Clothing styles all over Nigeria show the influence of the country's Arab neighbors. But each group favors a specific color or African pattern. Traditionally men wear a floor-length robe over matching baggy cotton pants. Hausa men usually wear white and embroidered robes, while the robes of Fulani men are pale yellow or light blue. Northern men also wear turbans to protect their faces from the heat and winds of the desert. The Yoruba robe, called an *agbada*, is usually light blue. Igbo men like to wear red patterned robes.

Northern women wear dark blue or black robes. An Islamic law requires the faces of Muslim women to be hidden from strangers, so they wear a covering on their heads that can be pulled across their faces. Fulani women wear a dark dress and large earrings—sometimes as many as six pairs! Yoruba women and girls wear a long skirt, called a wrapper, with a matching blouse and head scarf made from colorful cloth decorated with geometric patterns. Yoruba women are known for the unique ways that they tie bright turbans, called *gele*, around their heads. Around the waist, mothers may carry their babies in a wide, long piece of cloth called an *oja*. Igbo women wear simpler robes and wrappers than the Yoruba do, and, like the Igbo men, their clothes are usually dark red.

But not all Nigerians wear traditional clothes all the time. Sometimes they wear jeans and T-shirts.

(Opposite page) **These Yoruba men are dressed in the traditional *agbada*, loose pants, and hat.**
(Left) **A Nigerian woman who is carrying her baby in an *oja* stops to chat with a friend.**

Country and
City Life

In Nigeria the old and the new stand side by side. Traditional villages and towns, where most Nigerians live, are scattered throughout the country. Here the houses are made of wood or mud and usually don't have running water or electricity. In Yoruba villages, homes are arranged in groups of compounds or large yards, where cooking, bathing, and washing clothes take place. Narrow footpaths lead from one group of houses to another.

But many Nigerians live in apartments or small homes in urban areas. Lagos, the country's largest city, was built on an island in a **lagoon.** After the oil boom in the 1970s, many moved to Lagos to find work. The city expanded onto other islands and onto the mainland.

(Top) **Major highways run into the heart of Lagos, Nigeria's biggest city.** (Bottom) **In some areas, the mud walls that surround the old city in Kano have started to crumble.**

On Time

Whether in a village, a town, or a city, the pace in Nigeria is slower than it is in many other countries. "Nigerian Time" can be tough to get used to. No one seems to be in a hurry. If an invitation to a party says that it begins at 3:00 p.m., most likely things will be under way within an hour or two. Nigerian Time has been around for so long that it has become an accepted part of the country's culture.

Bridges connect the islands. Buses, trucks, bicycles, motorcycles, and people crowd the streets, creating traffic jams called "go slows."

The northern city of Kano, home to many Hausa, is actually divided in two—the modern city and the Old City. The modern city is a center for trade with countries from around the world. Non-Hausa Nigerians live in its Sabon Gari sector. The Old City, called the Tsohon Gari, houses the city's Hausa residents. Its huge walls, made of thick, solid mud, support 13 gates. The walls were originally built for protection against attackers. These days they separate the old from the new.

Family **Tree**

Nigerian families are closely knit. Mothers, fathers, brothers, sisters, grandparents, aunts, uncles, and cousins are part of one big **extended family.**

They all share a compound in a small town or village. (Extended families from the city usually don't live together because there isn't enough room in their apartments.)

A Yoruba man who lives in a small Nigerian village proudly poses with some of his wives and children.

All in the Family

Here are the Hausa words for family members. Practice these terms on your own family. See if they understand you!

father	uba	(oo-BAH)
mother	uwa	(oo-WAH)
uncle	kawu	(kah-WOO)
aunt	iya	(EE-yah)
grandfather	kaka	(kah-KAH)
grandmother	kakani	(kah-kah-NEE)
son	yaro	(YAH-roh)
daughter	yarinya	(yah-RIN-yah)
brother	dan'uwa	(dan-OO-wah)
sister	'yar'uwa	(yar-OO-wah)

There's an old African saying that it takes a village to raise a child. This is true in Nigerian villages, too. When parents work, all adults in the compound take turns watching the kids. And when grandparents become too old to care for themselves, their children or grandchildren tend to their needs.

Polygamy

Islamic law allows Muslim men to practice polygamy. That means that a man can be married to more than one wife at a time. So some families can be even bigger than the traditional extended family. A polygamous family shares a compound. The husband lives in one house, and each of his wives has her own home, where she lives with her children. Polygamy is not as popular as it once was. Most Nigerian families are made up of one husband, one wife, and their children.

Mosque, Church, or Altar

The majority of northern Nigerians, including the Hausa and the Fulani, are Muslims. Some Yoruba also follow the Islamic faith. Five times a day, Muslims pray to God, whom they call Allah. On Friday afternoons, Muslims leave school or work to go to the local mosque (house of prayer).

Most of Nigeria's Christians live in the south, where the Yoruba and the Igbo met Christian British missionaries in colonial times. In modern Nigerian churches, the prayer leader first says the Sunday service in English. Then an assistant translates the English words into the local Nigerian language. The audience also sings the hymns in one of the Nigerian languages.

Many Nigerians, especially those who live in the countryside, practice Traditional religions. Traditionalists

(Above) **Nigerians who practice Traditionalist religions pray at shrines like this one in southern Nigeria.** (Right) **A woman looks for a seat in a church in Benin City, a big town in southwestern Nigeria.**

believe in a great and powerful supreme God that cannot be worshiped directly. Instead people honor lesser gods such as Sango, the god of lightning and thunder.

Ancestor worship is also a part of traditional religion. Worshipers believe that ancestors are close to the gods and yet still close to the living. People ask for blessings from the supreme God through ancestors, who link the two worlds.

Holding his prayer beads, a Muslim (someone who follows the Islamic faith) prays in the northern city of Kaduna.

Many Nigerians combine Christian or Islamic beliefs with traditional religious ways. Some Nigerians might go to a mosque on Friday and to a church on Sunday. But then later on in the week, they may show respect for the supreme God by making an offering on the family shrine or on the shrine of a lesser god.

The Name **Game**

Nigerians love to celebrate! They begin going to parties at a very young age. Most don't even remember their first festive event—Ikomọ, their own naming ceremony. Here's how the Yoruba celebrate Ikomọ.

About a week after a baby is born, family and friends get together. The oldest member of the family prays for the new baby, sprinkling its mouth with a mixture of honey

What's in a Name?

Ada	(ah-DAH)	Igbo for "first daughter"
Jumoke	(joo-MOH-keh)	Yoruba for "everyone loves the child"
Kehinde	(KEN-day)	Yoruba for "second born of twins"
Taiye	(TIE-yay)	Yoruba for "first born of twins"
Uzoamaka	(oo-zo-a-MAH-kah)	Igbo for "the way is good"

(Left) **A woman in traditional dress cuddles her baby.**

(or sugar), water, and salt. Honey stands for the hope that the child's life will be sweet and good. Water represents the hope that the child will be as great as the ocean. And salt, which tastes bitter, is a reminder that life isn't always good. The leader passes bowls of the mixture around the room and all guests put dabs on their tongues. Finally the oldest family member announces the baby's name, which is usually taken from an ancestor. Everyone repeats the baby's name several times. The ceremony ends with a big party.

Luck Times Two

When Yoruba parents have twins, the family considers it good luck. That's a good thing, because more twins are born to Yoruba parents than to any other group of people in the world. The Yoruba believe twins are godlike and are in a hurry to get back to heaven. Parents carve, decorate, and leave offerings for a small sculpture called an *ibeji* to keep twins alive on earth.

Fish and **Yams**

For a country with millions of mouths to feed, the gathering of food is cause for celebration! For two days in February, the northeastern town of Sokoto holds the Argungu fishing festival. During the holiday, thousands of men and boys wade into the Sokoto River carrying nets stretched over bamboo poles. They use the nets to force fish into shallow water, where the fishermen scoop the fish into the nets. And get this, some of the fish weigh up to 150 pounds! The one who catches the biggest fish offers it to the organizer of the festival.

In Igbo towns and villages, people hold a festival to celebrate the yam harvest. This cousin of the sweet potato is the basic ingredient of many Nigerian foods. The party begins when the first yams are ready to be harvested, usually sometime

Using a mortar (the stick) and a pestle (the big wooden bowl), a woman mashes yams to make *fufu*, a food that kind of looks and tastes like mashed potatoes.

Men are allowed to fish for only 45 minutes during the Argungu fishing festival. Fishermen attach large gourds to the nets. The gourds keep the nets afloat if the fisherman accidentally drops his net.

in August or September. The village elder sacrifices a goat to start the festivities, and party-goers pour palm wine, a ceremonial drink made from palm trees, into the soil to honor their gods and ancestors.

For the next month, villagers eat—you guessed it—yams. Women and girls spend much of their time boiling, roasting, frying, or pounding yams for use in different recipes. Aside from gulping down a few yummy yams, young men from different villages challenge one another to wrestling matches, and girls sing and dance for an audience.

Hi Mom & Dad!
I'm having fun here in Nigeria. Today Grandpa and I went to Sokoto to watch the Argungu fishing festival—the only time when people are allowed to fish in the river. That's too bad, because some of the participants were catching really big fish! Men and boys wade into the river with nets. From the riverbank, I thought the fishermen looked like huge dragonflies! Later, we watched dancing and wrestling. The wrestling matches are a pretty big deal. Boys come from local villages to compete, and prizes are awarded to the winners.

See you soon!

Sum Mainitian
Waum Kaillim
Thaluurhu, Simlu
730N, Lauraithu

Time for **School**

Gi! That's "wake up" in Igbo. It's six o'clock on the first day of school—time for Nigerian kids to get up and get going. There's no problem figuring out what to put on. All children have to wear uniforms, even if they go to a public school.

On the first few days of school, Nigerian kids help clean the class-rooms and tidy the school grounds. Boys cut the grass and girls pull weeds from the dirt pathways. Inside the school, kids arrange the

Nigerian kids use brooms made from twigs to brush sticks and stones from the playground.

desks and chairs. On the following Monday, classes begin.

How would you like to leave school early each day? In Nigeria the school day lasts from 7:45 A.M. until 1:00 P.M. Students study a Nigerian language, English, math, social studies, art, religion, health, and physical education. School is fun, but it's also hard work. So each day after school, kids must finish their homework. After their sixth year, students have to take a tough final exam. If they pass, they earn a school leaving certificate. The certificate allows them to go on to secondary school or to leave school and start working.

Meet Thaddeus

He's from Aye-Ekan, a small village in southern Nigeria. Each morning, 13-year-old Thaddeus walks about a half an hour to St. Michael's Roman Catholic Primary School. At the end of this year, Thaddeus will take the final exam. He should do well on the math part of the test. Of all the subjects, he likes math best.

Shop 'Til
You Drop

When it's time to shop for food, most Nigerians will skip the grocery store and go to the open-air market instead. It's a great place to buy fresh fruits and vegetables, meat, fish, cloth, pottery, and almost everything else. The market is also a fun place to chat with friends.

In the crowded, narrow aisles that wind between booths, customers and shopkeepers haggle loudly over prices, while other vendors compete for your attention. One may say, "Customer, I have some fine cloth that will look very nice on you. Come in and take a look." Another vendor may interrupt by saying, "My own is better. Come and see."

With so much going on, it's amazing that shoppers are able to find what they need. But people selling similar goods are grouped in the same section. In the fruits and vegetables section, for example, tables are loaded with tomatoes, red peppers, onions, and green leafy vegetables. If you hear a lot of shoppers sneezing, that is probably the stall where a vegetable vendor is grinding red-hot peppers.

Vendors pile vegetables high on tables at this market in southern Nigeria.

Red-hot peppers are for sale at a market in Lagos. Nigerians grind up dried peppers and use the powder to spice up many foods.

Bargaining

All Nigerians, even children, are expected to bargain for whatever they want to buy at the market. The naira is the currency of Nigeria. It's divided into 100 kobos, just like the U.S. dollar is divided into 100 cents. Here's how it works:

Buyer: How much is that bunch of plantains?

Seller: Four naira.

Buyer: Four naira! That's too much money to pay for those few plantains.

Seller: What? Those are the biggest plantains of the season!

Buyer: (Shakes her head) No, I'm sorry, but I can't pay four naira.

Seller: How much do you want to pay for them?

Buyer: Two naira.

Seller: Give me three naira.

Buyer: How about two naira, 50 kobo? That's all I can pay.

Farther into the market, fruits of all kinds—mangoes, guavas, pineapples, oranges, and grapefruits—are piled high on the tables. The pleasant smell of spices lingers in other sections. Rice, beans, and even ground up crayfish are all sold in another area.

A *suya* vendor arranges the skewered meat around the fire to keep it warm.

Hot, **Hot, Hot!**

Drink plenty of milk during a Nigerian dinner, because the food is H-O-T, hot! One of the most popular afternoon or evening meals is a thick, spicy vegetable soup made with green vegetables, chopped onions, tomatoes, dried shrimp, and pieces of meat, fish, or chicken. Soup is usually served with *eba* (boiled cassava) or *fufu* (boiled yams). Both have the texture of bread dough or very firm mashed potatoes. They taste a little like mashed potatoes, too.

Ready to dig in? Don't worry about silverware. It's traditional to use your fingers to eat this dish. Nigerians roll a piece of the eba (or fufu) into a ball, dip it into the soup, and pop it in their mouths.

Between meals Nigerians don't go hungry. At roadside stands and at the marketplace, women and children sell cookies, candy, roasted corn, or fresh fruits. A special treat is *do-do*—plantain slices cooked in hot oil until they are golden brown. Suya—thin slices of beef seasoned with lots of spices, hot pepper, and ginger—is another Nigerian fast food. Cooks broil suya slowly over a fire and then skewer it on a stick with pieces of tomatoes and onions.

Mmmm! A Nigerian meal might include (from front left to right) *fufu,* **Jollof rice,** *do-do,* **spicy beans, thick vegetable soup, and grilled meat.**

DO-DO (FRIED PLANTAIN SLICES)

You will need:

One ripe plantain (cooking banana) It should be yellow and soft, but not squishy.

Salt to taste

3 tablespoons vegetable oil

Note: Don't try making this dish without the help of an adult!

1. Ask an adult to use a knife to remove the skin from the plantain and slice the plantain into thin, diagonal pieces.
2. If you'd like, sprinkle a little bit of salt on the slices.
3. Ask an adult to heat the oil in a skillet over medium heat. Use a fork to place plantain slices in the oil.
4. Cook for about five minutes on each side, or until they are golden brown. Use a spatula to flip the slices. Remove from heat.

Carved **Art**

Nigerian traditional art is famous throughout the world. Artists who lived in the powerful kingdom of Benin (located in southern Nigeria) during the 1500s produced bronze, brass, and ivory sculptures. These sculptures portrayed religious, historical, or royal subjects in fine detail.

Historically sculptors worked with whatever material was most readily available. In the north, where there are few trees, Hausa and Fulani artists used ivory, silver, and gold. In the east and west, ebony and ironwood trees provided durable wood for carving. After the British took over, they sent many of the oldest

(Above) **Hausa artists made this deep blue-and-white cloth. (Right) A sculptor chisels away wood to create a mask. A dancer will wear the mask in festivals and ceremonies.**

At the Kano dye pits, the artists tie knots in white cloth and dip it into dyes made with indigo, a plant that creates a deep blue color. After the cloth has dried, they untie the knots and use wooden mallets to hammer out the wrinkles. Vendors sell the cloth at the marketplace.

and finest sculptures to their art museums.

The ancient arts of carving and sculpting remain part of Nigerian culture. These days artists carve wooden masks that dancers wear at festivals and detailed historical scenes on wooden doors and gates. Artists sell their work at the market, in woodworking shops, and sometimes even by the roadside.

Do you like to dress up? Folks in Nigeria sure do! Earrings, necklaces, and bracelets are very popular. And Nigerian artists have a lot of materials for making jewelry, including silver and other metals, stones, beads, and wood.

They've Got **the Beat**

(Left) **Nigerian drummers pose at the Obi's Palace in Oyo. Drums are sometimes called "talking drums" because many Nigerians believe drummers can talk to the gods and to ancestors through drum beats.** (Below) **A man plays the bamboo flute.**

If you like to beat on a drum, then Nigeria's the place for you. The country has tons of drums—large, small, round, rectangular, or hourglass-shaped. Some drums are worn over the shoulder so that the drummer can play and walk at the same time. Drummers use their hands or sticks to beat the rhythm of the music.

If drums aren't your favorite, how about whistles, bamboo flutes, wooden xylophones, or gourd rattles? Don't want to play? Then just sing along and clap your hands.

The beat of the drum seems to get people of all ages on their feet. Teams of men and teams of women traditionally dance separately. There are even kids-only dances.

Different ethnic groups have their own music, dances, and costumes. On holidays and during festivals, musicians and dancers go from house to house dressed in colorful costumes, playing music and dancing. Many performers cover their faces with masks or wear bells around their ankles. Some dancers even walk on stilts!

Festival

You've probably worn a mask before—maybe for Halloween or as a character in a school play. In Nigeria dancers wear brightly colored wooden masks when they perform at festivals. The masked dancers represent different ancestors or gods and often appear at the end of a festival.

Story time

Long before there were any written languages in Nigeria, elders taught members of the younger generations about Nigeria's culture by telling stories. Most of these stories or folktales explained important ideas—where an ethnic group came from or how the world began. Storytellers were looked up to because they could remember the tales of long ago and could repeat them over and over—without mistakes!

The storytelling tradition is still alive in Nigeria. In villages people gather under trees to listen as storytellers thrill young and old with stories and myths of the people and the land. But Nigeria also has well-known modern authors. Ifeoma

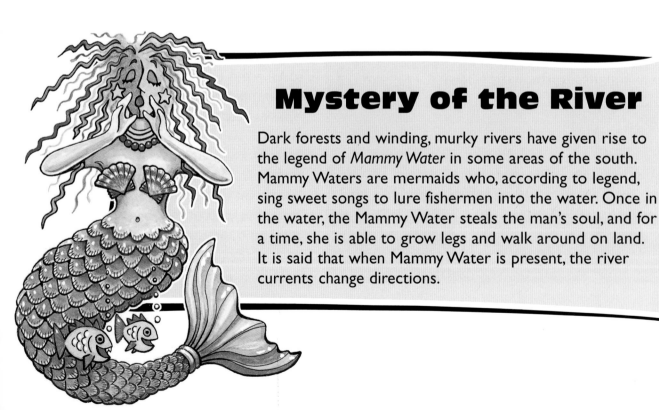

Mystery of the River

Dark forests and winding, murky rivers have given rise to the legend of *Mammy Water* in some areas of the south. Mammy Waters are mermaids who, according to legend, sing sweet songs to lure fishermen into the water. Once in the water, the Mammy Water steals the man's soul, and for a time, she is able to grow legs and walk around on land. It is said that when Mammy Water is present, the river currents change directions.

Onyefulu has written several fun books about Nigeria, including *A is for Africa*, *Emeka's Gift*, and *Ogbo: Sharing Life in an African Village*. Amos Tutuola's book, *Palm-Wine Drinkard*, is based on traditional Nigerian folktales and was the first Nigerian book to be praised outside Nigeria. Chinua Achebe has written several popular novels, including a very famous one called *Things Fall Apart*.

Long ago Nigerians carved pictures to tell stories. In this carving, the Three Wise Men bring gifts to the baby Jesus.

Between 1500 and the mid-1800s, European slave traders captured millions of Africans, forced them onto ships, and took them to North and South America, where they were sold as slaves. Nigerians and other West Africans weren't allowed to take any personal belongings, but they managed to take the folktales they could remember. Stories like those about Brer Rabbit, which remain popular in the United States, originally came from Nigerian oral tradition. Called *Wakaima* in Nigeria, Brer Rabbit is a small, helpless creature who always outsmarts bigger, stronger animals. To slaves, who had no control over their own lives, Brer Rabbit's adventures gave them hope.

Kids play soccer during gym class.

Soccer **Rules!**

Although swimming, wrestling, boxing, table tennis, track and field, and other sports are popular, THE number-one sport in Nigeria is soccer. Nigeria's national soccer team, the Green Eagles, won the gold medal at the 1996 Summer Olympic Games in Atlanta, Georgia. The National Stadium in Lagos, where the Eagles play, is one of the most modern sports stadiums in Africa.

In Nigeria soccer is a game for the young and the old. Kids join soccer clubs at an early age. School and club teams meet regularly to play matches. When they outgrow their soccer shoes, Nigerians become loyal fans of the sport. Not only do Nigerians like to play and watch soccer, they like to read about it, too. Newspapers usually include two or three articles about soccer each day.

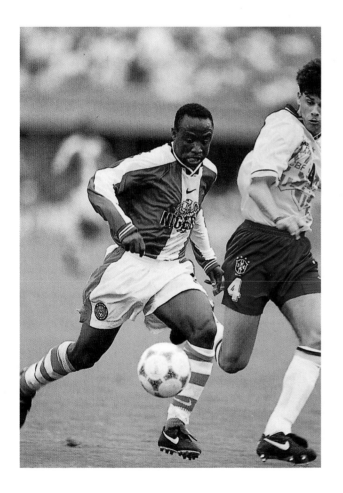

(Above) **A Nigerian fan wears the colors of his team during the Olympic game against Argentina.** (Left) **During the 1996 Olympics, a player for the Green Eagles moved the ball down the field as a Brazilian player closed in. Nigeria beat Brazil 4 to 3 in overtime.**

Kicking **Back**

Nigerians love to go to the movies. Action-packed U.S. films, Chinese martial-arts films, and Indian films of love and adventure are big favorites. And sometimes the audience is more fun to watch than the movie! When something sad happens on screen, the theater is filled with sobs and hisses. During exciting scenes, the audience claps, shouts advice, and sometimes even pretends to duck blows and dodge bullets. Movie-goers yell their feelings throughout the entire movie. It's all part of going to the movies in Nigeria!

After school kids usually play outside until it gets dark. Favorite games include hide-and-seek and hopscotch. When it does get dark, kids go inside and may decide to play *ayo*, a game that is popular in many parts of Africa. The aim of the game is to move seeds around a tray in a certain way so as to end up with as many seeds as possible.

Two kids play ayo using a board carved from wood. Ayo is also called *mankala*, *kigogo*, and *oware*. All mean "transferring." There are many ways to play ayo, too. Try our version on the facing page.

Have Fun!

Try making your own Ayo board and then follow the rules listed below.

You will need:
- 2 empty egg cartons • Transparent tape • Scissors
- 48 markers—use dried beans, small pebbles, or marbles.

Make the Board

1. Cut 2 egg cups from one of the egg cartons.
2. Attach 1 egg cup to each end of the other carton with tape.

Play the Game

1. Place the board between 2 players so that the end cups are to the right and left. A player owns the 6 closest cups and the end cup to the right. Players store any markers they win in these end cups. Put 4 markers in each of the middle 12 cups.
2. The younger player starts by picking up 4 markers from any one of the cups. The player works toward her end cup, dropping one marker into each cup along the way. When she reaches the last cup on her side of the board, the player drops a marker into her end cup.
   - If she drops the last marker of her turn in her own end cup, she gets to go again.
   - If she has more markers left to drop, she drops them one at a time into cups on her opponent's side of the board, beginning with the cup next to her end cup and working to the left. (She may even drop a marker in her opponent's end cup, which he then gets to keep.)
3. Player 2 repeats step 2 with markers from one of his cups.
4. When players drop the last marker of their turn in one of their own empty cups, the player wins all of the markers in the cup next door on their opponent's side. Players put these winnings in their own end cup. When one of the players' 6 middle cups are empty, that player wins the game. The winner is the player with the most markers.

Several traditional homes, like these built from mud and straw, make up a family compound.

Glossary

colony: A territory ruled by a country that is located far away.

desert: A dry, sandy region that receives low amounts of rainfall.

ethnic group: A large community of people that shares a number of social features in common such as language, religion, or customs.

extended family: Mothers, fathers, brothers, sisters, grandparents, aunts, uncles, and cousins. In Nigeria, extended families often live together in one household.

harmattan: Winter wind that blows off the desert in West Africa.

lagoon: A shallow pond or channel connected to a larger body of water.

savanna: A tropical grassland where annual rainfall varies from season to season.

tributary: A stream feeding a larger stream or lake.

tropical rain forest: A dense, green forest that receives large amounts of rain every year. These forests lie near the equator.

In 1967 the Igbo declared their independence from Nigeria and created a new nation called Biafra. The Nigerian government fought to keep the country together in a civil war. Biafra surrendered in 1970, after many Igbo had died.

Pottery is popular in Nigeria. This woman is shaping a large pot, which she will later use to carry water.

Pronunciation Guide

Abuja	ah-BOO-jah
agbada	ahg-BAHD-ah
Argungu	ar-GOON-goo
Benin	beh-NEEN
Benue	BEN-way
Cameroon	kahm-ah-ROON
ẹkabọ si	en-KAH-bor see
Enugu	en-OO-goo
Fulani	fuh-LAH-nee
gele	GAY-lay
gi	JEE
Guinea	GIH-nee
harmattan	har-mah-TAN
Hausa	HOWS-ah
Igbo	EE-boh
ibeji	ee-BEH-jee
Ikomọ	EE-kom-or
Lagos	LAY-gohs
Lokoja	low-KOH-jah
Niger	NEE-jur
Niger River	NEYE-jur
Nigeria	NEYE-jee-ree-yah
oja	OH-jah
Sabon Gari	SAH-buhn GAH-ree
Sango	shan-GOH
Sokoto	soh-KOH-toh
suya	SOO-yah
Tsohon Gari	SOH-nan GAH-ree
Wakaima	wah-KAY[ih]-mah
Yoruba	YOH-row-bah

Further Reading

Adeeb, Hassan and Bonnetta. *Nigeria: One Nation, Many Cultures.* New York: Marshall Cavendish, 1996.

Anda, Michael O. *Yoruba.* New York: The Rosen Publishing Group, Inc., 1996.

Azuonye, Chukwuma. *Edo: The Bini People of the Benin Kingdom.* New York: The Rosen Publishing Group, Inc., 1996.

Buettner, Dan. *Africatrek: A Journey by Bicycle through Africa.* Minneapolis: Lerner Publications Company, 1997.

Koslow, Philip. *Benin: Lords of the River.* New York: Chelsea House Publishers, 1996.

Koslow, Philip. *Hausaland: The Fortress Kingdom.* New York: Chelsea House Publishers, 1995.

Lester, Julius. *The Tales of Uncle Remus: The Adventures of Brer Rabbit.* New York: Dial Books, 1987.

Nabwire, Constance and Bertha Vining Montgomery. *Cooking the African Way.* Minneapolis: Lerner Publications Company, 1988.

Nigeria in Pictures. Minneapolis: Lerner Publications Company, 1995.

Onyefulu, Ifeoma. *Ogbo: Sharing Life in an African Village.* New York: Gulliver Books, 1996.

Temko, Florence. *Traditional Crafts from Africa.* Minneapolis: Lerner Publications Company, 1996.

Metric Conversion Chart

WHEN YOU KNOW:	MULTIPLY BY:	TO FIND:
teaspoon	5.0	milliliters
Tablespoon	15.0	milliliters
cup	0.24	liters
inches	2.54	centimeters
feet	0.3048	meters
miles	1.609	kilometers
square miles	2.59	square kilometers
degrees Fahrenheit	5/9 (after subtracting 32)	degrees Celsius

Index